Where I Live

My City

by Meg Gaertner

FOCUS READERS
SCOUT

www.focusreaders.com

Focus Readers is distributed by North Star Editions:
sales@northstareditions.com | 888-417-0195

Produced for Focus Readers by Red Line Editorial.

Photographs ©: iStockphoto, cover, 1, 9 (bottom), 13 (top), 13 (bottom), 15, 16 (top left); Shutterstock Images, 4 (top), 4 (bottom), 7, 9 (top), 11, 16 (top right), 16 (bottom left), 16 (bottom right)

Library of Congress Cataloging-in-Publication Data
Names: Gaertner, Meg, author.
Title: My city / Meg Gaertner.
Description: Lake Elmo, Minnesota : Focus Readers, [2021] | Series: Where I live | Includes index. | Audience: Grades K-1
Identifiers: LCCN 2019054759 (print) | LCCN 2019054760 (ebook) | ISBN 9781644933367 (Hardcover)) | ISBN 9781644934128 (Paperback) | ISBN 9781644935644 (eBook PDF) | ISBN 9781644934883 (Hosted eBook)
Subjects: LCSH: Cities and towns--United States--Juvenile literature. | Human settlements--United States--Juvenile literature. | Readers.
Classification: LCC HT123 .G24 2021 (print) | LCC HT123 (ebook) | DDC 307.760973--dc23
LC record available at https://lccn.loc.gov/2019054759
LC ebook record available at https://lccn.loc.gov/2019054760

Printed in the United States of America
Mankato, MN
082020

About the Author

Meg Gaertner is a children's book editor and author. She lives in Minneapolis, Minnesota. When not writing, she is usually dancing or spending time outside.

Table of Contents

1007

Many Communities

My city has many neighborhoods.

People live in these places.

I meet my **neighbors**.

I become friends with them.

neighbors

Many Areas

My city has many shopping places. People buy food at a **grocery store**. They see movies at a **theater**.

grocery store

theater

My city has many parks.

My friend and I

go to a park.

We play at the park.

Many People

My city has many people.

Some people drive in cars.

Some people take the **bus**.

ONLY
car
SPEED LIMIT 30

bus
M2 VIA 5 AV
M2 VIA 5 AV
125
Limited
6705
122
6380
6380

I love to walk around.

I love to see my city.

Glossary

bus

neighbors

grocery store

theater

Index